A sensitive and biblical framew... to give to youn... grapple with d... people especially and their leaders to read then discuss the book's content, using the questions at the end of each chapter. Read then share the book's message with others.

Eryl Davies
Research Supervisor, Union School of Theology
Church Elder, Heath, Cardiff

The troubled mental health of young people is now almost daily news, and we urgently need practical, accessible and biblical resources to help the rising generation. Providing wise pastoral advice which is both realistic and well founded in scripture, this short book is an ideal starter, both for personal use and for youth group discussion.

Jonathan Lamb
Writer, teacher, and minister-at-large for Keswick Ministries

As a biblical counselor, I'm always looking for that resource on depression that is clear, insightful, hopeful, compassionate, and short enough to be readable, yet long enough to provide real and practical help. With all the things in this broken world that press down on us, it's hard to imagine anyone who couldn't benefit from John Kwasny's scripturally-sound guidance. I will certainly recommend it for our church's counseling library.

Janice Cappucci
ACBC certified biblical counselor and author of *Storm Clouds of Blessings: True Stories of Ordinary People Finding Hope and Strength in Times of Trouble*

This wonderful little book is full of practical scriptural wisdom. As an experienced biblical counselor, Dr. Kwasny offers a well-balanced and comprehensive perspective on depression. His writing is clear, easy to read, and full of hope. He covers a lot of important ground in relatively few pages. While this resource is aimed at teens, I would happily give it out to counselees of all ages.

Jim Newheiser
Director of the Christian Counseling Program, Reformed Theological Seminary, Charlotte, North Carolina
Executive Director, The Institute for Biblical Counseling and Discipleship (IBCD)

JOHN C. KWASNY

SERIES EDITED BY
JOHN PERRITT

A STUDENT'S GUIDE TO DEPRESSION

Scripture quotations are from *The Holy Bible, English Standard Version,* copyright © 2001 by Crossway Bibles, a publishing ministry of Good News Publishers. Used by permission. All rights reserved. ESV Text Edition: 2011.

Copyright © John Kwasny 2022

paperback ISBN 978-1-5271-0797-7
ebook ISBN 978-1-5271-0866-0

10 9 8 7 6 5 4 3 2 1

First published in 2022
by
Christian Focus Publications Ltd,
Geanies House, Fearn, Ross-shire,
IV20 1TW, Great Britain
www.christianfocus.com

with

Reformed Youth Ministries,
1445 Rio Road East
Suite 201D
Charlottesville,
Virginia, 22911

Cover by MOOSE77

Printed by Bell & Bain, Glasgow

All rights reserved. No part of this publication may be reproduced, stored in a retrieval system, or transmitted, in any form, by any means, electronic, mechanical, photocopying, recording or otherwise without the prior permission of the publisher or a licence permitting restricted copying. In the U.K. such licences are issued by the Copyright Licensing Agency, 4 Battlebridge Lane, London, SE1 2HX www.cla.co.uk

CONTENTS

Series Introduction 7

Introduction 9

1. Pressed Down 15
2. More Than a Feeling 21
3. On a Downward Spiral 29
4. Losing It 37
5. Crossing the Line 43
6. Avoiding Pain 49
7. Staying the Course 55
8. The Anger Beneath 61
9. The Anxiety Beneath 67
10. Joy to the World 75

Appendix A: What Now? 81

Appendix B: Other Resources on this Topic ... 85

Series Introduction

Christianity is a religion of words, because our God is a God of words. He created through words, calls Himself the Living Word, and wrote a book (filled with words) to communicate to His children. In light of this, pastors and parents should take great efforts to train the next generation to be readers. *Track* is a series designed to do exactly that.

Written for students, the *Track* series addresses a host of topics in three primary areas: Doctrine, Culture, and the Christian Life. *Track's* booklets are theologically rich, yet accessible. They seek to engage and challenge the student without dumbing things down.

One definition of a track reads: *a way that has been formed by someone else's footsteps.* The goal of the *Track* series is to point us to that 'someone else' – Jesus Christ. The One who forged a track to guide His followers. While we cannot follow this track perfectly, by His grace and Spirit He calls us to strive to stay on the path. It is our prayer that this series of books would help guide Christ's Church until He returns.

In His service,

John Perritt
RYM's Director of Resources
Series Editor

Introduction

Depression. What is the first thing that comes to mind when you hear that term? A mental disease? A psychological disorder? A spiritual problem? Something that only weak-minded people experience? An emotional issue common to all people? Whatever you believe about depression at this point in your life, hopefully you understand that it is not easy, and can be very confusing. Whether you are struggling with depression yourself, or you have a friend or family member who battles it, then it is worth your time to learn more about it. Depression is not a problem that should be ignored or downplayed in any way. It deserves our serious attention and requires competent help.

There is a growing recognition of depression and other mental health issues in our culture today. In previous generations, to admit to being depressed was seen as admitting weakness, or simply part of your character – think of 'Eeyore' in *Winnie the Pooh*, or Puddleglum for fans of *The Chronicles of Narnia*. Fortunately in the West today many people are encouraging open conversations about mental health. Even the British royal family, once a symbol of the 'stiff upper lip' attitude!

The truth is, ever since sin and death entered our world, human beings have struggled with all sorts of physical, emotional, mental, spiritual, and relational problems. Therefore, from the earliest of times, people have tried to figure out how to solve these problems—with varying degrees of success. But, even today, various types of professionals are still seeking solutions and attempting to help people with diverse kinds of problems. Depending on who you ask or seek help from, you will be given differing information on the causes of problems as well as how to fix them. This goes for the problem of depression too.

So, where and to whom should you go to get a better understanding of your own depression or the struggles of someone close to you? Of all the information out there, this book will uniquely ground the problem of depression firmly in a biblical worldview. As Christians, we believe that God's Word has been given to us as our highest authority of truth for all of life. The apostle Paul states it this way: 'All Scripture is breathed out by God and profitable for teaching, for reproof, for correction, and for training in righteousness, that the man of God may be complete, equipped for every good work' (2 Tim. 3:16-17). The Bible speaks to the issues of human life, and trains us to live in ways that grow us in grace, and please and glorify God.

The Word of God, then, is our best starting point in understanding depression. From there, other knowledge and wisdom that fits within a biblical worldview of problems can be useful. Since God created you, who better can teach you what is going on in your heart, mind, soul, and body? Human beings are made in the image of God—a reflection of who God is and how God works. Yet, we humans are also born in sin, which mars that image and affects every part of our being. To make matters worse, we all live in a fallen, sinful world, surrounded by sinful people and all sorts of conflict and difficulties. The Bible teaches us the truth about our condition in its stories of real people and real situations, as well as in its practical theological instruction.

But, thankfully, we don't just learn about the bad news of our problems in Scripture. We human beings may be lost and dead in our sins, but we are redeemable. As Jesus Himself said: 'For God so loved the world, that He gave His only Son, that whoever believes in Him should not perish but have eternal life' (John 3:16). Salvation is found in Christ alone, by God's grace alone, through faith alone. Then, there's more good news: Salvation comes with the gift of the Holy Spirit, who works powerfully with the Word of God to transform us into the likeness of Christ. That means we have the God-given power, wisdom, and ability to deal with the problems of this life, including a challenging one like depression.

As will be more thoroughly discussed in the following chapters, having a biblical understanding of depression is the essential foundation for real, long-lasting change. It is the key to solving this problem of mind, heart, soul, and body. But that doesn't mean it's easy, or that Christians won't struggle for years with the problem of depression. Knowledge must be connected to wisdom, fueled by the work

Introduction

of the Holy Spirit in our hearts and minds. We also need other people in our lives to talk with, to counsel us with the truth in love, and to walk with us through difficult places. Finally, the problem of depression demands that we pay attention to both body and soul, and to things inside and outside of us too.

If you are discouraged about this lingering or recurring problem in your life, hopefully the Lord will use this book to encourage you. If you have questions about the causes and contributing factors to the problem of depression, then prayerfully, you will find answers here. If you want to be able to offer words of wisdom to a friend or family member weighed down by depression, then this is also the resource for you. Since depression is a universal problem that impacts people of all ages, backgrounds, and ethnicities, it is well worth your study even if depression isn't really on your radar just yet. And, as Christians, it is vital that we have a view of human problems that is firmly rooted in God's Word and God's ways.

So, are you ready to get some practical, biblical help with the problem of depression? It may not be the most exciting thing on your agenda, but it just may be one of the more important efforts right now. Take your time. Interact with the material as well as the Scripture behind it. Answer the reflection questions at the end of each chapter. You may even want to find someone to study it with you. At the end of the book, there is a list of other helpful resources on depression, as well as some next practical steps to take in the process. May God bless you and give you His grace as you grow in your understanding of the problem of depression and its solutions.

1. Pressed Down

A friend sends you a text message with just three words: 'I'm so depressed!' How do you respond? Maybe you simply text back, 'What's wrong?' Then, the words begin to flow. You may read a story of lost love, a hopeless view of the future, or a state of seemingly endless physical or emotional suffering. Unfortunately, your friend's declaration can be misused, such as in statements like: 'I'm so depressed that my team lost the championship.' But in many other cases, real pain shines through—possibly even in a text that says: 'I want to kill myself.'

So, let's ponder a problem that appears to be so prevalent in our world today: What exactly is depression? Before getting more technical, consider the literal use of the term: To be depressed is to be 'pressed down.' If you think about it, that's really a good word picture. When a person is depressed, he or she is collapsing under a weight—a heavy burden that is unbearable. To use another common phrase, depression feels like a person is 'carrying the weight of the world on her shoulders.' Being in this state brings untold pain, suffering, and misery.

Or, maybe you have heard the phrase: 'being down in the dumps.' This is another vivid picture of depression. If you are in the 'dumps,' you are surrounded by all sorts of garbage; you are part of a huge trash heap. You may have never had the privilege of touring your local city dump, but it certainly isn't a place in which you want to hang out for very long. Being in that sort of pit would only drive you to despair, as you gaze around at what your life has become. Just think of the prodigal son and his life of feeding pigs in the pigpen to get one more image of depression in your mind (Luke 15:11-32).

The problem of depression, then, has many universal features to it. Here are the main symptoms that are shared by all who suffer with it:
- Fatigue
- Pessimism and hopelessness
- Pain

- Trouble concentrating, making decisions
- Difficulty sleeping or sleeping too much
- Persistent sadness
- Overeating or appetite loss
- Loss of interest in pleasure
- Suicidal thoughts.

Depression is described as sucking the joy out of life, as being a stubborn darkness that will not go away. It has a way of sticking around as an unwelcome visitor in our lives. In the *Harry Potter* series, the author imagines fearful creatures called dementors, invisible beings who feed on happy emotions. J.K. Rowling drew on her experience of depression to describe them: 'They infest the darkest, filthiest places, they glory in decay and despair, they drain peace, hope, and happiness out of the air around them.'[1] Depression is scary!

Medical and psychological professionals have given diagnostic labels to various types of depression; yet, they all share many of the same symptoms. A helpful way to think about it, as with many other problems, is that depression has a spectrum or a range to it. Some people experience a mild depression

---

[1] J.K. Rowling, *Harry Potter and the Prisoner of Azkaban* (London: Bloomsbury, 1999), chapter 10.

that comes and goes, while others have more intense depressed feelings that never seem to go away. There is seasonal depression, as well as depression related to a particular event or situation. Some depression is chronic (lasting a long time), while other depressions are acute (brief in nature). Whatever the particular type, depression is a difficult problem that requires a proper understanding and solution.

At this point, you may be wondering: Can a Christian be depressed? That's a really good question. Some Christians believe that once someone is saved, and enjoys all the blessings of a relationship with Jesus Christ, all major struggles (like depression) should end. After all, followers of Jesus should always be joyful, right? Christians also have access to the fruit of the Spirit—love, joy, peace, patience, and so on. Since the person who is depressed is hopeless, pessimistic, persistently sad, and even has suicidal thoughts, it just seems so opposite of the life of the believer in Jesus!

While Christians certainly do enjoy life in Christ, and the power of the Spirit and the Word, we still have ongoing difficulties in this world. Think about it this way: Do Christians have things in their lives that are 'pressing down' upon them? Definitely! Difficult relationships, complicated life events, and hard decisions can be weights on our shoulders. Physical and mental diseases, disabilities, and disorders can press us down as well. Then, there's the work of Satan, the attacks of this evil world, and our own sinful hearts that produce heavy burdens. So, yes, Christians get depressed too, requiring help and care that will provide the possibility of change.

As will be discussed further, the Christian who is suffering with depression has resources that the non-Christian does not have. Truthfully, those who are outside of Christ have reasons to be depressed all the time! Life in this fallen world is always pressing down on us, and none of us are strong enough in and of ourselves to withstand it. Between our own sinful hearts, the lies of the devil, and the temptations found throughout our present culture, it is no wonder depression is regularly at the top of the charts of human problems.

Thanks be to God, He has given us new life in Jesus Christ and the sanctifying work of the Holy Spirit. Some of the most familiar words of invitation from Jesus to the lost soul are found in Matthew 11:28-30. They are a great comfort for those suffering from depression as well:

Come to me, all who labor and are heavy laden, and I will give you rest. Take my yoke upon you, and learn from me, for I am gentle and lowly in heart, and you will find rest for your souls. For my yoke is easy and my burden is light.

Main Point

Depression is a universal problem that unbearably presses many of us down.

Questions for Reflection

- What things are bearing down on you right now?
- What do all the symptoms of depression have in common?
- Why is it misguided to think that Christians should never get depressed?
- What resources does the Christian have to deal with the problem of depression?

2. More Than a Feeling

Has anyone ever asked you the following question – *How are you feeling?* I'm sure they have. If not, let me ask you right now, how are you feeling? Take a minute to think of how you might answer that question honestly. That question can be a little challenging for various reasons.

Believe it or not, some people don't recognize they are depressed—or how deeply depressed they really are. When finally discussed, a person struggling with depression typically describes it with 'feeling' words. 'I have just been feeling so down and discouraged lately.' 'I have felt so bummed out for a long time.' 'I feel utterly hopeless about life.' Depression certainly is a problem of our feelings, or our emotions. So, one of the plainest ways to describe this problem is to say: 'I have depressed feelings.'

DEPRESSION

But where do those depressed feelings come from? Why are some of your friends or family depressed? Now, that's a big and important question! To put it simply, our feelings are connected to what is happening inside of us, as well as outside of us. Things that happen externally are much easier to understand, so we'll start there. If your best friend punches you in your face, how will you feel? After the initial shock, I'm guessing you'll feel a combination of anger and sadness! Everything that happens to us evokes a certain feeling. While many of our feelings change quite quickly, some will linger for some time.

Now, let's move inside in order to understand our feelings. Since God has created us as a unity of body and soul, feelings are connected to our bodies. It's important to draw distinctions between our body and soul, but also realize the unity God's Word places on them. As Sam Allberry says, 'Where we use the word soul to mean our inner or spiritual life in contrast to the physical body, the Bible typically means something much more all-encompassing. In both the Old and New Testaments, the main words we tend to translate as 'soul' mean the whole person, not just the non-physical part of us.'[1] While there's a clear distinction between the body and soul, we must be cautious of separating them too often because there's a beautiful unity between them and one will impact the other.

Some of you may think of the internal workings of your body if you have ever taken an anatomy and physiology class. You know that our amazing bodies have an intricate system of chemical, hormonal, and biological processes underneath the surface. When it comes to the problem of depression, you may have heard that it is caused by a shortage of a certain chemical—or some type of 'chemical imbalance.' While that is a possible cause, it is not always the whole story. Being made in the image of God, human beings are more than just the sum total of our body chemistry. And our emotional problems do not develop solely from a mishap in our chemical processes.

Yet, it would be a mistake to ignore the physical causes that contribute to our feelings of depression. Certain diseases of the body can definitely create depressed feelings. Depression can also result from a particular physical or

---

1 Allberry, Sam. *What God Has to Say About Our Bodies: How the Gospel is Good News for Our Physical Selves* (Wheaton, IL: Crossway Books: 2021), 42.

mental disability. If you think about it, your physical state will always have an impact on your emotions. How do you feel if you haven't had a good night's sleep for several days? What if your diet has consisted solely of pizza and fast food for months? How does the lack of regular exercise affect your emotions? Any and every breakdown in the health of your body will have some consequences on your feelings.

Now, take a minute to go back to that initial question – How are you feeling? Think about that in light of some of the factors we've just described. Are you dealing with a physical illness right now? Have you had lack of sleep? Lack of physical exercise? What have you been putting into your body? Think about all of these factoring into the question and how they are impacting your feelings.

But there is more going on inside of you than just chemical and biological processes. You have been given a mind that is able to think. When you feel, there is a thought that is connected—most often preceding it by a split second. After your best friend punches you in the face, you have a thought—or, two or three. 'What in the world just happened?' 'How could he/she do that to me?' 'I didn't do anything to deserve that!' Do you see how those thoughts would produce either sadness or anger—or later, even depressed feelings? What we think about, or where our minds go, also contribute to how we feel.

A biblical understanding of the human being brings us even further and deeper inside than just our bodily processes and our thoughts. Each one of us also has a heart—not our physical blood pump, but that inner self, the 'real you.' According to Jesus, it is from within our hearts that arise our thoughts, behaviors, and feelings (Mark 7:14-22). Because our hearts are sinful, they can produce all sorts of evil thoughts and sinful behaviors that, in turn, lead to bad feelings. A heart that has not been changed by the power of the Spirit and the work of Christ will only produce sinful things. Since Christians have a changed heart, we have the new ability to think rightly, and act in godly ways, potentially resulting in good feelings. This does not mean that a Christian's 'good actions' aren't ever tainted with sinful motives or that unbelievers can't ever do anything virtuous. While we can't dig too deeply into this specific area, simply keep in mind that our actions do impact our feelings.

So, a good way to understand depression is to begin with what is happening at the 'feeling level.' When you are depressed, you will feel sad, angry, anxious, or a combination of those and other emotions. Then, you must look at what is happening in the 'doing level.' What are you thinking? How are you behaving? What words are you saying? Your thoughts, actions, and words all impact the way you are feeling. But don't stop there. Ask God to go to work on your heart. If you are a Christian, your heart has already been changed and cleansed. Yet, as we will discuss further, even the Christian struggles with idols of the heart that need to be demolished. All your life, you will need to have your heart renewed and re-formed.

But don't forget that feelings of depression are also the result of what is happening inside your physical body as well as outside in your world. If you are worried that your feelings are depressed, irrational, and persistent, it is important to have a physical examination by a medical doctor. A doctor can also counsel you about whether or not medication would be helpful. Even if you're not quite sure how you're feeling, it's important to voice that to someone. Oftentimes depression is described

More Than a Feeling

as a fog that clouds our thinking; therefore, you need someone else to help you think clearly.

Even if you receive medical attention for your depression, any good doctor will tell you that you also need to address the things going on in your world—your relationships, activities, stressors, and situations. These contribute to how you are feeling as well. A good Christian counselor[2] can help you with those things on the outside, as well as what is going on inside your heart and mind.

Do you see how depression is more than just a feeling? There are many causes and contributing factors that can produce those complicated depressed feelings. But there is one last way to understand depression as more than a feeling: It is really a mood. Moods are persistent feelings, or an ongoing state of our minds and emotions. This fact alone is why depression is often called a 'mood disorder' and not just a feeling problem! This does not mean that the physical or external factors causing depression will always be obvious.

---

2   I wrote 'good Christian counselor' for a reason. Sadly, there are many poor Christian counselors out there. Some of the advice given can hardly be labeled 'Christian'. It is important that your parents and pastors help you in choosing a good counselor.

While there may be other factors, this can be a helpful way to explore the depression you, or a loved one, is dealing with.

Main Point

Depression is a mood disorder that is connected to your body and soul, heart, and mind.

Questions for Reflection

- In what ways is depression more than just a feeling problem?
- What things on the 'outside' can produce depression?
- What can break down on the 'inside' that may result in depression?
- Why is it essential to recognize that humans are both body and soul?

3. On a Downward Spiral

What are some of your favorite Old Testament stories? Think about some of the well-known stories you heard over and over when you were growing up. Perhaps you remember some of the coloring sheets you'd always color in Sunday school. Or, some craft you'd bring home that would end up on your parent's refrigerator… until it would strangely disappear one day.

One of the more memorable tales of the Old Testament is the story of Jonah the prophet. Who could forget a true story of someone swallowed alive by a big fish, only to be vomited out three days later? Of the many applications of this incredible story, one that is often missed is the emotional roller coaster Jonah rode with the Lord God. Think about it for a moment. Jonah is called by God to preach to the Ninevites, the enemies of Israel. Jonah takes a boat and sails the opposite way, rebelling against God. Then, there's the storm that ended when Jonah was thrown overboard. After spending three days in the belly of the great fish, Jonah praises God and was ready to get a second chance to obey Him.

But that wasn't the end of the roller coaster. Jonah preaches the coming wrath of God to the Ninevites, and they do the unthinkable: repent and turn to God in humility! When God forgives, and relents from destroying Nineveh, the emotional ups and downs continue, bringing Jonah to become angry and bitter. By the end of the story, I would suggest that Jonah is deeply depressed. Jonah's own words to God were: 'It is better for me to die than to live… Yes, I do well to be angry, angry enough to die' (Jonah 4:8-9). Jonah is a great example of what happens when you end up on, not just an emotional roller coaster, but on a downward spiral. It typically ends up in the problem of depression.

Let's break it down to help us understand the process. Picture a downward spiral: round and round it goes, like a corkscrew, or maybe a spiral staircase leading to the basement. The downward spiral of depression begins with a problem, which leads to a poor response,

On a Downward Spiral

then spirals down to an associated problem, and then another wrong response. Over and over this pattern continues until the pit of depression is reached. Each mental, emotional, or behavioral response just complicates things, leading to more problems.

Now, back to Jonah. Here's one way to diagram how he became depressed:

- Original problem: God calls Jonah to Nineveh.
  - Emotional response: Jonah doesn't want to go. He hates the Ninevites.
  - Sinful response: Jonah gets on a boat that goes the opposite direction.
- New problem: God sends a storm that may kill Jonah and the entire crew.
  - Response: Thinking his life is over, Jonah asks to be thrown overboard.
- New problem: Jonah is swallowed by a big fish. (God saves his life.)
  - Response: Jonah prays and repents.
- Original problem (again): Now that Jonah is saved, he still has to go to Nineveh.
  - Response: Jonah preaches to the Ninevites.

- ◇ Emotional response: Jonah growing in anger. He doesn't want to see them saved.
- New problem: God graciously saves Nineveh from destruction.
  - ◇ Emotional response: Jonah is even more angry. Now he just wants to die.
- Jonah is now depressed.

Then, in Jonah 4, God seeks to teach His prophet about the foolishness of his anger, showing him how great His mercy is. Unfortunately for us, the story ends without any information about Jonah's response to God. Does his anger and depression subside, or persist? Does he move off the downward spiral or continue on it? Whatever the case, hopefully you see how easily we can descend into depression when we do not respond well to the things happening in our lives. Sinful responses and poor choices contribute to a deepening mood disorder that becomes harder and harder to escape.

Have you seen this downward spiral occur in your life? Say you're struggling to deal with that break-up or friendship loss, which means you can't concentrate so your grades are slipping, you're then irritable at home and feel like you're constantly disappointing your

On a Downward Spiral

parents. Maybe your situation is different, but can you think of a time when problems just seemed to pile up on each other?

From our vantage point, it is easy to rebuke Jonah for his errors, showing him that he is totally to blame for his depression. 'Jonah, you're a prophet of God. You should do exactly what God commands you.' 'You should know better than to rebel against God. You can't run away from Him!' 'Why are you so angry that God saved Nineveh? Shouldn't you be happy that they are not evil anymore?' We could go on beating Jonah up with shame and guilt, couldn't we? Now, there is no doubt that he brought on many of his problems. He, like all of us, must be held responsible for sinful responses that kept him on the downward spiral of depression.

But, it is essential to recognize that it is not an easy thing to jump off the downward spiral. We can't know what was truly going on in Jonah's heart and mind, just like no one really knows yours. Jonah certainly had some righteous anger, since the Ninevites were an evil, vicious people who destroyed the lives of innocent people. It's never easy seeing your enemy not get what he deserves! Even though

Jonah misunderstood the character of God, it is understandable that it depressed him to see God forgive wicked people. In many ways, things happened so fast – like life often does – that Jonah could have truly been overwhelmed by his emotions.

Thankfully, the downward spiral of depression is not the end of the story. By God's grace, there is an upward path that enables the Christian to climb out of the pit of depression. Depression does not have to be the final destination. Understanding how one has descended on that spiral leads to wisdom on how to take an upward path. New decisions must be made. Difficult thoughts, attitudes and feelings must be acknowledged. People need to be forgiven. Humble repentance and submission to the will and work of God in our lives must occur. When you find yourself at the bottom of the downward spiral, look up to the God of all mercy and grace!

Yet, while the above is a glorious truth, it's important to know that there's not always a quick fix with depression. If the above helps you to move beyond the type of depression you're dealing with – praise God! But don't beat yourself up if it doesn't. As was said earlier, depression is on a spectrum, so there are many causes. Keep looking to the God of grace, talk with your parents and a counselor and know you're not alone in the midst of your struggle.

Main Point

Depression may occur at the end of a downward spiral.

Questions for Reflection

- How did Jonah contribute to his own problem of depression?
- What things outside of Jonah contributed to his depression?
- Have you ever realized you were on a downward spiral? What happened?
- How can the Christian who is depressed begin on the upward path?

4. Losing It

You just lost your keys, and you are late for class. How do you feel? Your phone has gone missing. What thoughts are running through your mind? Losing things that are important to us typically produces feelings of anxiety, fear, frustration, anger…or all the above. Could you imagine yourself being happy or excited if you lost something valuable? The reality is that no one enjoys or celebrates a loss—unless it doesn't really matter that much. Loss is another one of the facets we need to understand concerning the problem of depression.

Now, you probably won't find yourself depressed after losing your keys, or even your cherished phone. But what happens when those losses begin to accumulate? Experiencing loss after loss has the potential of producing depressed feelings. But, then, there are much more significant losses that would have an even greater impact. The loss of a friendship. The loss of a loved one to death. The loss of reputation. The multiple losses that occur when disease or disability strikes. The perceived loss of future success. In this world, there is much to lose—significant things that may never be regained. So, again, loss can easily produce depression.

Let's imagine that you are at the funeral home, visiting a friend who has just lost a loved one. What is the most immediate emotion your friend is feeling? Sadness? Yes. Sorrow? Yes. But the best word to describe his or her emotional response is GRIEF. Grief is that deep sadness or sorrow that is experienced after a significant loss, especially one caused by death. While visiting at the funeral home, would you put your arm around your friend and say, 'Hey, stop being so sad. You don't need to grieve. This is no big deal. Be happy!'? I hope not. If you did express anything close to those sentiments, you may have just lost a friend!

What this scenario is intended to illustrate is that grief is the normal response to loss. God has designed us to be sorrowful when we lose something or someone of great value. Tears are God's gift that flow when our hearts are burdened with sadness and grief. When we don't grieve over sad situations, then there is something terribly wrong. Think about the Lord Jesus. Did He ever experience deep sorrow and grief? In John 11:35, we get to see Jesus weeping over the death of His friend, Lazarus. He was also grieving over the reality of the destruction of sin and death in this world. In Luke 22, we read of Jesus in deep anguish of soul before going to His own death on the cross. As fully God and fully man, Jesus grieved deeply over loss. Since we are made in the image of God, grief is part and parcel of our humanity.

So, what does grief have to do with depression? There are at least two things to consider.

First, what people think is depression may actually be normal sorrow and grief. You wouldn't label your friend who just lost a loved one as depressed, would you? It is expected that grieving should go on quite some time after experiencing loss of life. But there are other things that should produce grief that don't cause true depression. You should grieve over your sins which produce a loss of fellowship with God. You should grieve over a loss of a friendship. You should even grieve over the state of this evil, fallen world. Grief over the right things may go on for some time. We must be careful not to confuse this 'good grief' with depression.

But then there is grief that later turns into depression. When has a person been grieving over something or someone too long? That's a tough question. Yet, common sense says that there is a time for grief to end and happiness to return. So, grief that is prolonged can grow into a stubborn depression. It may be extended because the person really isn't dealing well with the particular loss. Or, instead of trusting and believing in God's good purposes, His character is questioned and His ways are rejected. It should be understandable that grief can turn into depression, since loss is so painful. We need to take great care to grieve well and deal with loss biblically in order to keep from plunging into the depths of depression.

There is one other thing to think about when it comes to loss, grief, and depression: grief tells us about what we value the most. Grieving over the death of a loved one communicates that you greatly valued him or her in your life. That's a good thing. But there are some things we can value too much—things that become idols to us. Things we over-value will produce ungodly grief, and potentially, depression. On the other end of the spectrum, there may be things we should grieve over that we don't value enough—like the consequences of our sin. One thing you may need to work on is valuing more highly the things that God values, and de-valuing things that are not truly important.

What sets Christians apart is that we aren't people who grieve without hope (1 Thess. 4:13). We will go further into the subject of hope in our next chapter. When encountering the problem of depression, it's important to examine the losses that may be involved. They may be obvious, like some of the ones already mentioned. But they may be less clear and more under the surface, like the loss of security, loss of innocence, or the loss of direction. We can even lose perspective on many things in life that can produce grief and depression. Ask the Spirit to show you what you have lost, followed by the truth of what you have gained. As a Christian, you can deal with losses with the gospel reality of all that you have in Christ (Phil. 3:8)!

Main Point

Loss, sorrow, and grief may lead to depression.

Questions for Reflection

- Why is it good to grieve?
- When can grief turn into depression?
- What can grief show us about the idols of our hearts?
- How should Christians respond to losses in this life?

5. Crossing the Line

Have you ever been told that you have 'crossed the line?' Maybe a friend says: 'Most of the time, your teasing is pretty funny. But this time you have crossed the line.' Or, one of your parents may tell you: 'Your behavior has been pretty bad lately. But your most recent stunt has crossed the line.' What are your friend and your parent saying? *Your words or your actions have gone too far.* You have entered the 'danger zone.' And, typically, crossing the line comes with some sort of negative consequence. Your friend may not want to talk to you for a while. Your parent may discipline you in a more severe way. Crossing the line is most often not a good thing.

Another way to understand the problem of depression is that it occurs when sadness has 'crossed the line.' Remember, sadness is a normal emotion that God has given us.

Living in a fallen world among sinful people as a sinful person brings many opportunities to be sad. Sadness will be with us as Christians until we get to heaven, where there will be no 'mourning, nor crying, nor pain anymore...' (Rev. 21:4). So, you will be sad at times. You will get down and discouraged. As long as you don't cross the line, you will not be depressed.

So, what's this 'line' that turns sadness into depression? I would suggest there are actually two lines, or maybe two parts to this line. The first one was mentioned in the last chapter: the 'hope line.' A person who is depressed often becomes hopeless—they lose hope in God, people, and often life itself. Now, it is understandable to lose hope in people or a particular person, since people fail one another all the time. And, it makes sense to lose hope in what is happening in life, since we live in a world that is broken by sin. Putting our hope in ourselves, other people, or in this world will end up producing hopelessness at times in our lives.

The real problem is when we lose hope in God. But let's stop right there and make sure we understand what hope is—as God's Word defines it for us. Hope is not just a wish, as in

'I hope I get a pony for Christmas.' True hope isn't crossing our fingers and 'hoping for the best.' Biblical hope is desiring something good to happen in the future with the confidence that it will happen! This is why the only sensible hope begins with putting our hope in God.

The Psalmist expresses it this way: 'Why are you cast down, O my soul, and why are you in turmoil within me? Hope in God; for I shall again praise him, my salvation and my God' (Ps. 42:11). Do you hear how he was depressed, and needed to cross back over that 'hope line?' And the only way to move forward was to first hope again in the Lord.

Putting your hope in God begins when you turn from your sins and profess saving faith in Jesus Christ our Lord. But, even after becoming a Christian, your hope in God can waver. As you experience trials, pain, suffering, and difficulties, you may be tempted to lose confidence in God. He may seem uncaring, unloving, distant, or impotent. But the truth to hold onto is that it makes no sense to lose your hope in God! When you read and study God's Word, you learn that God always keeps His promises (Heb. 10:23). He can always be counted on to do what is right (Heb. 6:10).

Jesus will never leave you or forsake you (John 14:18). Hope in God increases in our lives as Christians when we put our eyes more on God than on our circumstances!

Please don't hear me saying this is another quick fix. Placing our hope in God is a daily struggle, especially when faced with, seemingly, unanswered prayers. It's no surprise that Scripture often refers to these in terms of warfare. I'm sure you've heard someone say, 'It's such a battle to have hope' – it's easy to feel that the good times will never come back! As our world has been confronted with Covid-19, a lot of us have learned that extended times of hardship have a negative effect on our ability to hope. While it can be hard to have hope don't let that discourage you from engaging in the battle.

So, what's the other line, or part of the line, that is crossed in depression? The 'trust line.' Again, it is normal to lose trust in people, because they can be very untrustworthy. Putting your trust in this world is also a foolish thing to do. Believe it or not, it is also not very wise to trust in yourself—in your own abilities, knowledge, or personality. Actually trusting in imperfect people, the world, or yourself may set you up to become depressed! Look at how the prophet Jeremiah describes this crossing of the 'trust line':

Thus says the LORD: 'Cursed is the man who trusts in man and makes flesh his strength, whose heart turns away from the LORD. He is like a shrub in the desert, and shall not see any good come. He shall dwell in the parched places of the wilderness, in an uninhabited salt land.' (Jer. 17:5-6)

Even though Jeremiah doesn't use the word 'depression,' the vivid imagery used to describe this person certainly reminds us of this problem. The man who trusts in man, or in himself, has crossed the line from trusting God. His heart actually turns away from God in this choice to trust something or someone else. The crossing of the trust line produces a shriveled-up life, a life with no pleasure or good—a desert experience. This Scripture passage helps us to understand how a turning away from trusting a trustworthy God will potentially produce depression, as we wander in our own wilderness.

You may be thinking: 'Okay, so I have crossed the line. I have lost hope in God. I don't trust Him to love me and lead me anymore. What do I do now?' Great question! Just asking it puts you on the upward path out of the pit of depression. Confessing to God where we are in our minds and hearts is a big step. To move forward, we need the Spirit's help to grow in hope and trust—to regain confidence in what God is doing in our lives. Ask for that help, seek God in His Word, and watch what happens. By God's grace, you can cross that line again, as you pray with the Psalmist: 'Hope in God; for I shall again praise Him, my salvation and my God.'

Main Point

Depression comes as we cross the hope and trust lines.

Questions for Reflection

- Why is it so tempting to cross the 'hope' and 'trust' lines?
- Why doesn't it make sense to lose hope in God?
- What things do we trust in rather than in God?
- What steps must we take in order to cross over to the right side of the line?

6. Avoiding Pain

Someone once said: 'No pain, no gain.' From the first time that statement was uttered until now, these words have been repeated all across the world, especially in gyms, workout areas, and sports locker rooms. We get what it means, right? It takes hard and often painful work to be able to have success in this life. To have good times, you often have to suffer through the hard times. The great things in this life are only gained if we are committed to do whatever it takes. I don't know about you, but I'm not a big fan of this concept. Why can't it be: 'No pain, all gain' instead? Why must we human beings go through painful things in this life?

If you are someone who actually enjoys pain, and seeks to have as much pain as possible enter your life, then that's another problem. Really, no sane person desires pain—

not even the extremely competitive athlete. He or she just knows physical pain is part of the process of gaining strength, or victory. That same person would probably avoid emotional pain or relational pain, if at all possible. The point is: Pain is an undesirable guest that we hope never comes, and can't wait until it leaves. Painful situations are not something we typically seek after or look forward to, and we breathe a sigh of relief when they are over.

So, how does pain relate to depression? As has been already discussed, pain and suffering can create feelings of depression. Physical pain, mental pain, and emotional pain all lead us down that downward spiral to the pit. Then, we know that depression itself is painful. Being depressed hurts, stings, and even numbs. The reality is that none of this sort of pain connected to depression seems to bring any 'gain.' Hopefully, no one you know is encouraging the experience of emotional pain in order to produce some sort of gain in your life. Can God use the pain of depression for your good? Definitely! As the apostle Paul says, 'for those who love God all things work together for good' (Rom. 8:28). But again,

Avoiding Pain

depression isn't a state of heart and mind that anyone truly wants.

Therefore, when you are depressed, it makes sense that you want to be relieved of your depression as soon as possible. While it may appear that some people enjoy being stuck in the depths of depression, it is just not true. What is important to know is that there are some things we do that actually prolong depression, rather than help to solve it. On the top of that list is the desire to avoid all pain— to never be hurt again. I know, we just said that it is normal to avoid pain. But, people can actually avoid pain too much, becoming overly committed to not having pain ever again. Whether they realize it or not, extreme pain avoidance ends up making their depression more painful and more persistent.

Let's flesh this problem of 'pain avoidance' out a bit more. A girl in your class, Andrea, has struggled making friends for years. She is socially awkward, and can even be obnoxious at times. Andrea shares with you that she has been depressed for years, and regularly battles suicidal thoughts. Tired of being hurt all the time, she has committed herself to just be alone forever, not caring about anyone. Andrea proclaims that she will always be single, and that is the end of the matter. Do you think this approach to life will solve her depression? The truth is that Andrea will only experience more pain as she tries to numb it by avoiding future relational pain. It just won't work.

Then, there's Bob. Bob is frustrated by his inabilities and failures. He couldn't make the football team, which has been his dream for years. Even though he studies more than most of his friends, he can't make the good grades he desires. Bob looks at his future and sees nothing but hardship and pain. So, he resolves to never dream again. What's the point? Dreams don't come true anyway. Success will always elude him. Why work so hard when he will fail anyway? Do you recognize Bob's avoidance of pain? Will it solve his depression? Is this a good definition of the victorious Christian life? It may seem to be a sensible way to deal with his pain, but it will only produce more heartache in the end.

Hopefully, you get the idea. More importantly, it is essential to see how tempting a commitment to pain avoidance is—especially to someone who is depressed. It is not helpful to simply condemn Andrea or Bob, and tell them to stop avoiding their pain. And please don't tell them (or yourself), 'no pain, no gain,' in these types of scenarios. Satan, the great Deceiver, would love for us all to check out, band-aid the pain, and try to avoid all future struggles and difficulties. But God often uses mental, emotional, and relational pain to wake us up from our spiritual slumber. He also uses pain to make us more dependent on Him and His strength. Ultimately, He allows pain in the life of the Christian to shape us and mold us to be more like Christ. While this is true, it is important to know that God hates to see His children suffer. He cares about your tears, He cares about the pain in your life. Remember that He took the pain of humanity on Himself in the incarnation of His Son, Jesus. He did this to put an end to sin, an end to suffering.

The truth is that no one can successfully avoid pain in this life, as has been said many times so far. Rather than avoid pain, the believer must turn to the Lord in his or her pain. For a believer with depression, this will mean opening up to a counselor or trusted adult about the issues causing pain and hopelessness. Trying to control the amount of pain that enters our lives denies that God is in control of our lives. It is a fruitless effort because we are not powerful or strong enough. But God is. He is the only One who can bring the relief we require. He is the only deliverer and rescuer. Instead of running from the pain, run to the Cross of Jesus, where the ultimate price was paid for all the pain of sin and death!

Main Point

Avoiding pain typically prolongs and intensifies depression instead of solving it.

Questions for Reflection

- What makes depression such a painful experience?
- Why is it tempting to try to avoid pain at all costs?
- What do we really gain when we experience emotional, mental, and relational pain?
- Why does God allow pain into our lives?

7. Staying the Course

Have you ever run in a race? Maybe you're on the cross country or track team at your school and you compete in races with some frequency.

Running is a fairly common activity and is even used as a metaphor for the life of a Christian. Several times in the New Testament, the Christian life is compared to a race (1 Cor. 9:24, Gal. 5:7, Phil. 3:14, Heb. 12:1-3). More specifically, it is described as a marathon rather than a sprint—a race that tests our strength and endurance. Running a marathon is not easy, and finishing it is even harder. It takes training, discipline, patience, and high motivation to run in such a way as to win. A race, like the Christian life, has a starting point and a finish line—and is designed to be a trial of perseverance. 'Staying the course' is one way of communicating the need to run the race of life well, and finish strong.

When people experience a depressive disorder, it makes running the race of life overwhelming. Depression itself tells us just to quit, to stop the race. Thoughts like: 'It's just not worth it,' 'It's all so meaningless,' and 'I'm just so tired of it all' can dominate the mind. Of course, Satan would love nothing more than for Christians to drop out of the race, to not finish well. When everything seems hard, and the burdens are just pressing down, who wants to keep running anyway? It is just so tempting to sit the race out, to refuse to participate, to take off our running shoes, and just go home.

The ultimate 'quitting' the race for those who are depressed is suicide. As has already been said, recurring suicidal thoughts are one of the symptoms of the problem of depression. While some people who are depressed just want to 'take a break' from the race of life, others become more determined that a permanent exit from this world is needed. Over the course of depression, suicide can become more and more attractive. It can feel like a solution to the hardship and struggle of the race. Suicide can actually end up looking like the best possible way to escape every obstacle that has appeared in the race.

Staying the Course

So, what can you do when you have suicidal thoughts?

The most important thing is to talk to someone about what you are thinking and feeling. This may be really hard. You may be embarrassed and ashamed to share that you are struggling with suicidal thoughts and depressed feelings. Yet, during these times, it is essential to have a strong network of relationships that can help—through prayer, counsel, comfort, and encouragement. Sometimes, friends and family members may be the best ones to help a person with suicidal thoughts. At other times, a Christian counselor may be necessary. Talking out what is bouncing around in your head is one of God's methods of healing and change.

A network of support will be able to help you work out mental tools to respond to suicidal thoughts:

First, God's Word tells us to take every thought captive to the Lordship of Christ (2 Cor. 10:5). Christians are to think on things that are true, noble, right, pure, lovely, and admirable (Phil. 4:8). Therefore, you can best take hold of suicidal thoughts by asking yourself questions like:

Is this thought true? Is it right? Does it please God? Is it consistent with what God's Word says about me, God, and life? Is it pure? Is it beautiful, or ugly? When our sinful and harmful thoughts aren't captured and submitted to Christ, they can take over and rule our actions. Christians are always in the processes of renewing our minds in Christ Jesus.

A **second** way to deal with suicidal thoughts is to talk to yourself rather than listen to yourself. As was mentioned previously, depression has a way of 'talking' to us—telling us to quit this race of the Christian life. Depression often produces a harmful level of passivity, where the person spends an inordinate amount of time listening to various voices in his head. In this state, listening to these thoughts will only produce more depressed feelings. So, it is essential to learn to talk to yourself, to tell yourself the truth to combat all the lying voices. Theologians often talk about the importance of 'preaching the gospel to yourself every day.' Truthful talking to ourselves is an active force that can dispel some of the darkness of depression. [1]

---

[1] This is something Martyn Lloyd-Jones discusses in his book, *Spiritual Depression*. It may be a challenging read for some, but it is helpful.

Along the same lines as talking to yourself, a **third** weapon against suicidal thoughts is being careful about what is filling your mind. The passivity and darkness of depression can make any activity in the race of life seem impossible. So, it is easier just to fill our minds with meaningless media, television shows, movies, music, and social media offerings that can make things worse. Many people who are depressed stop reading their Bibles, and stop listening to sermons or other forms of Bible teaching. But it is essential to feed our minds with truth, with beauty, with the glorious things of God to combat suicidal thoughts. As difficult as it may be, even starting small with a portion of the Psalms or a brief devotional can help a person stay the course.

While depression calls on people to surrender, to wave the white flag, and to quit the race, God lovingly commands us persevere and finish well. Sometimes, depression can keep us focused so much on the past and present that we fail to see the road ahead. Even when we look at it, it seems murky, dark, and scary. But for the Christian, Jesus is our light on the path. As the writer to the Hebrews says, we are to keep our eyes on Jesus, 'the founder and perfecter of our faith, who for the joy that was set before Him endured the cross, despising the shame, and is seated at the right hand of the throne of God' (Heb. 12:2). We can stay the course of life and persevere, because our Lord Jesus has persevered for us!

Main Point

Depression tells us to quit. God calls us to persevere in Christ!

Questions for Reflection

- In what ways is the Christian life like a marathon race?
- Why does depression make us want to quit this life?
- What are some practical ways to combat suicidal thoughts?
- Why is Jesus essential to staying the course of life?

8. The Anger Beneath

Two brothers. Both made an offering to God. One offering was accepted, the other was rejected. From this real-life conflict came the very first murder in human history: the killing of Abel by his brother, Cain. How could something so incredibly evil like this happen? What leads a person to murder his very own brother? Unfortunately, we are not given a lot of information in the Bible, so we can't really get into Cain's head. Yet, we do have these words: '...but for Cain and his offering he had no regard. So Cain was very angry, and his face fell' (Gen. 4:5). It's a dark picture: in the face of rejection, Cain becomes sullen, jealous, and 'very angry'. Instead of responding in a godly way, Cain becomes a tragic figure in an extreme example of what can happen when depressed moods result from internalized anger.

Many years ago, one of my professors defined depression as 'anger turned inward.' Let's unpack this idea briefly by using the Cain and Abel example again. Anger typically begins with a problem—a trigger event that evokes a sense of injustice. For Cain, the rejection of his offering coupled with Abel getting blessed created angry thoughts and feelings. Instead of working to solve the problem he had with God and his brother, Cain's anger turned inward for a time and fueled a descent into what could be called a state of depression. Finally, that anger turned outward into murder.

You'll be pleased to hear that not all depression leads to the murder of another person. Yet, it is important to discover whether or not anger is below the surface. A person who is depressed could be angry at God. He or she may be angry at a specific person or even people in general. It could be anger about a particular situation. Or, it may be a generalized anger at life itself. When sinful anger is not turned to solve the problem or deal with the person, it can be stuffed down deep inside. As that anger mutates into bitterness, it can join itself with sorrow. And that combination will end up producing a depressed mood.

This progression has often led me to counsel people with this observation: 'You aren't just depressed. You are really angry as well!'

Say your dad loses his job for some reason that isn't his fault. He's been looking for work for months now, but can't seem to get a lucky break. Over time the accumulation of rejection emails and phone calls affect his moods, making him irritable and sullen. He seems angry at the whole world.

God's Word has much to say about anger. Which biblical principles will help us keep from allowing our anger turn into depression? First, it is vital not to let our anger fester for days and days on end. The apostle Paul puts it this way: 'Be angry and do not sin; do not let the sun go down on your anger' (Eph. 4:26). Staying angry for days, weeks, and even months will draw us into that downward spiral of depression. God has given us the emotion of anger to produce essential energy to solve problems. But our anger becomes sinful as it hangs around for a long period of time. So, working to deal with the anger in a prompt manner, by God's grace, can keep it from creating depressed feelings.

Another way to keep our anger from morphing into depression is to replace it with kindness and forgiveness. Again, the apostle Paul writes: 'Let all bitterness and wrath and anger and clamor and slander be put away from you, with all malice. Be kind to one another, tenderhearted, forgiving one another, as God in Christ forgave you' (Eph. 4:31-32). When we are angry, we say unkind words, think vengeful thoughts, and plot sinful actions. To reverse course, Christians must allow the Holy Spirit to soften the heart so kindness and forgiveness can flow. When problems that produce anger are resolved by forgiveness, it will be easier to avoid sliding into depression.

A third truth about anger is found in the Book of James: 'Let every person be quick to hear, slow to speak, and slow to anger; for the anger of man does not produce the righteousness of God' (James 1:19-20). Learning to be slow to anger keeps anger from coming out inappropriately in our words and actions. Building a habit of being quick to anger can also foster depressed feelings. In other words, if you are constantly getting angry over things big and small, it is likely you will more easily become depressed. By the work of the Spirit, we are to slow down in our anger, listen and think more carefully, and seek to promote the righteousness of God. By dealing with anger in a godly way we can stop anger settling inward.

There is one final form of anger that must be addressed when it comes to depression: anger towards self. Of all the people to become angry at in this life, anger that is directed toward self is almost guaranteed to produce depression. If anger at another can lead to murder, it should make sense that suicide (self-murder) is preceded by anger at self. We don't have the space here to discuss all the reasons people become angry at themselves. The important thing to understand is how to best deal with that anger. Some would say you have to forgive yourself. But the better way is to express your anger to God, confess what is sinful in your thinking, and seek His forgiveness. Then rest in Him, knowing that He has forgiven you and welcomes you into His arms. Remember, the anger of man does not produce the righteousness of God—and it can also lead to the complicating problem of depression.

Main Point

Beneath the problem of depression often lurks unresolved anger.

Questions for Reflection

- Why can unresolved anger easily turn into depression?
- What does God's Word say about how to deal with our sinful anger?
- For what things can you become angry at God?
- In what ways can you become angry at yourself?
- Once again, if you are having suicidal thoughts, it is vital that you share them with an adult. A parent or guardian, a pastor, a teacher, a coach or a counselor. Please don't keep these thoughts to yourself.

9. The Anxiety Beneath

Another problem that goes hand-in-hand with depression is the problem of anxiety. If you do an internet search for the most common problems experienced by young people, you will find depression and anxiety as numbers one and two on the list. So, what's the connection between these two issues? Does a person struggle with anxiety and then get depressed, or does a person who is depressed tend to become more anxious about life? Yes, and yes.

These two problems feed into each other and interact with each other in ways that exacerbate the other. That said, anxiety is similar to depression in that it falls on a spectrum. Just as there are multiple factors that can feed depression, there are multiple ways in which one could be anxious. Since there's only so much space in this book, every nuance cannot be covered. But you need to know that finding success in changing either problem will often help the other as well.

Let's begin with the more typical case in which anxiety is producing depression. In the same way that anger can lie beneath depression, anxiety can be the root problem that needs to be addressed. An anxious heart produces anxious thoughts and actions, which then ends up creating depressed feelings. So, in order to properly solve the problem of depression, there must first be an admission and understanding of the anxiety that lies beneath. Anxiety, as you may already know, is what is produced when we are working overtime to control what we can't control in this life[1]. When it becomes more of a way of responding to anything and everything, an anxiety disorder can lead down the spiral to depression.

Here's an example of how anxiety can be the initial problem that ends up producing depression. Imagine you are from a family that has always struggled with having enough

---

1   For more on anxiety, check out Dr. Edward T. Welch's book in this series, *A Student's Guide to Anxiety* (Fearn: Christian Focus Publications: 2020).

The Anxiety Beneath

money. Your parents are always behind on the bills, and not able to afford basic needs, making life in your home very stressful. As the oldest child, you have always been more keenly aware of these financial problems. So, you have become anxious about money as well. The problem is, you can't do much to fix the problem. All you can do is look forward to the day when you can leave home and take care of yourself. In the meantime, you worry about your parents' ability to pay for your college, a car for you, and other needs you have. It all starts to feel so sad, overwhelming, and hopeless!

Does that help you to see how anxiety can produce depression? The key is that when an anxious person becomes hopeless and overwhelmed, there comes a sense of resignation that produces depressed feelings. It should make sense that if you cannot do anything to fix what you are anxious about, you will end up losing hope in that situation. So, in the above example, what change needs to happen? If your parents got their financial act together, that would sure help. But, if they never do, you would be responsible to deal with that anxiety. Only when you become less anxious about your present and future circumstances would you become less depressed.

So, what are some ways to address the problem of anxiety?

RECOGNIZE THINGS THAT TEMPT YOU TO BE ANXIOUS

Sure, there are some people who are anxious about everything. But most of us have very specific things that tempt us to worry. It may be your financial situation, or your future. You may worry a lot about certain relationships, or relationships in general. Then, there is anxiety over what people think or how to act in certain situations. There are an endless number of things that produce anxiety. Understanding what produces anxiety allows you to solve them better, seeking help from the Lord.

RECOGNIZE HOW YOUR ANXIETY IS ATTACHED TO A DESIRE TO BE IN CONTROL

When we can't control the things we want to control, anxious thoughts and feelings will result. Giving up your need for control is a very hard thing. Yet, as Christians, we know that God is in control of all things! Instead of trying to be

The Anxiety Beneath

God, strive to let God be God. Yes, this means that the anxious person struggles with trusting God in particular areas of life. In the Sermon on the Mount, Jesus taught that being anxious is the opposite of believing that God will take care of all the things we need (Matt. 6:27-34). In the end, Jesus says that being anxious will not add even a single hour to our lives. It only takes away our peace and joy in the hours we have been given.

RECOGNIZE HOW PRAYERLESSNESS CAN BE CONNECTED TO ANXIETY

The apostle Paul gives us another biblical practice when we are struggling with anxiety: 'Do not be anxious about anything, but in everything by prayer and supplication with thanksgiving let your requests be made known to God' (Phil. 4:6). If you think about it, when you are anxious you are often not praying. You are certainly not thanking God for the situation! So, in order to combat anxiety, you must make a conscious effort to stop and pray, asking the God who is in control to handle your problem. But these prayers must always be coupled with praise, giving thanks for however God chooses to deal with your situation. Again, it comes back to whether or not you will trust God to be in control.

Much more could be said about handling anxiety biblically, but it is beyond the scope of our subject. Hopefully, it helps to understand that depression can be the result of other problems that need to be confronted. Remember, depression is most often an indicator, a warning light that alerts us to things that are not going right in the heart and mind. An overly anxious mind can produce depression. A longstanding problem that provokes us to anxiety, with the additional component of hopelessness, will bring about depressed feelings. So, don't ignore your anxious heart. Don't see it as just a normal part of how you are wired. When Jesus tells us not to be anxious, He knows the Christian doesn't have to be. We have a God in control, a God who provides all we need, and a God who perfectly loves us in Jesus Christ!

Main Point

Beneath the problem of depression often dwells an anxious heart and mind.

The Anxiety Beneath

Questions for Reflection

- Why do you think depression and anxiety are the most common problems experienced by people your age?
- How can anxiety end up producing depression?
- What things most often tempt you to become anxious?
- What is the best way you can combat your anxiety?

10. Joy to the World

What does the person who is depressed need the most? If he or she is not a Christian, then the right answer would be 'Jesus!' Since our greatest human problem is the fact that we are lost and dead in our sins, our greatest need is for a Savior. But, what if you are a Christian struggling with depression? One possible answer to this 'greatest need' is 'happiness.' After all, depression is deep sadness, right? And the opposite of sadness is happiness. So, when you are depressed, it would make sense that you really need to be happy.

Actually, there is a better answer, as you may have guessed from the title of the chapter. The person who is depressed needs JOY. Joy is what is most lacking in his or her life. Now, you may be thinking: Aren't happiness and joy just two different words for the same thing? We certainly tend to use them interchangeably.

But, even though they are similar, happiness and joy are really quite different. While we often want to simply be happy in this life, God calls us to, and can give us, a deeper and more substantial joy.

Let's consider a few key differences....

JOY IS MORE THAN AN EMOTION

Happiness is an emotion; joy is an attitude of the heart. Thankfully, God has given us the ability to feel—to have emotional responses about what's going on inside and outside of us. Happiness is the emotion that comes when things are generally going well in our lives. It would actually be very strange to be happy when something bad was happening! But joy is an attitude of the heart based on the security of knowing that our lives are fully in God's hands, and He has 'blessed us in Christ with every spiritual blessing' (Eph. 1:3). An attitude is a settled way of thinking that directs what I do and say. This definition makes joy much deeper than happiness, coming from the 'heart level' of self rather than just the 'feeling level.' This also means joy is not dependent on good circumstances or happy things.

JOY IS A CHOICE

Happiness just happens; joy must be chosen and counted. Now, to be clear, happiness is not something magical that just appears all on its own. God has designed us as a complex combination of body and soul; so, there are chemical, physiological, mental, and spiritual processes that contribute to bringing about happiness. But happiness 'just happens' in the sense that it is experienced almost immediately when something good happens. You don't really have to think about it. Joy, on the other hand, is a conscious, thoughtful choice. You must choose to be joyful, even when the circumstances are sad—and worse than sad. James puts it this way: 'Count it all joy, my brothers, when you meet trials of various kinds, for you know that the testing of your faith produces steadfastness' (James 1:2-3). At times this can seem like an impossible command! Joy may only come after a time of learning to trust in God's goodness, strength, and love for you. And part of our joy comes from knowing that our hope is in heaven: 'For this light momentary affliction is preparing for us an eternal weight of glory beyond all comparison' (2 Cor. 4:17). The Bible says that even the worst trials will seem 'light' in retrospect, when compared to the glory awaiting us.

JOY IS A GIFT

Happiness is self-generated; joy is a fruit of the Spirit. God has made people to have both good and bad feelings. So, happiness comes from within self—something every human being can feel. If you are depressed it may feel like you can never be happy again, but this is not true. The ability to become happy is still there, even though it is covered over by depression. Joy, on the other hand, is a gift from God, a fruit of the work of the Holy Spirit in your heart. In Galatians 5:22, Paul puts joy on the list of spiritual fruit. That means, we must ask God to give us His joy in our hearts. And, it also means that joy comes as we grow in the Lord, and walk with the Spirit in this life.

JOY IS FOCUSED ON OUR CREATOR

Happiness is often situation-centered or self-centered; joy is God-centered. We love to be happy, because it says that things are well and good in our own universe. While you certainly can be happy for other people, happiness is first about self. That's why it is easier to be happy for a friend's success than an enemy's good fortune!

Joy to the World

So this truth makes happiness focused more on yourself and your circumstances. Joy, on the other hand, has its sights on God. In Nehemiah 8:10, we read: 'And do not be grieved, for the joy of the LORD is your strength.' Joy is given by the Lord, and it is designed to be directed to the Lord. You will only be truly joyful when your eyes are fixed on Jesus, and your heart is tuned to the Lord.

JOY IS NOT FLEETING

Happiness comes and goes; joy is long lasting. If feelings of happiness are based on good situations and circumstances, then it should make sense that they are not designed to stick around. No one can be happy all the time, because life isn't always good. Various forms of suffering are always present in this fallen world. If you know someone who is always happy, it is most likely true joy. Joy can persist in our hearts, by the work of the Spirit. Our hearts can be filled with joy on a regular basis. Yet, since we are sinners, joy can also come and go. As we grow in Christ, joy can become a regular feature of our lives.

Hopefully, by reading this book, you have not come to the conclusion that solving the problem of depression is an easy process. 'Just find joy in the Lord,' is not to be proclaimed as some mantra or quick solution. You must be compassionate and understanding towards those with depression, as well as be patient and humble when you are the person struggling. Yet, as a Christian, you do have spiritual resources that can lead you out of the pit of depression to finding joy in the Lord again. As Jesus told His disciples: 'These things I have spoken to you that my joy may be in you, and that your joy may be full' (John 15:11). When we have true joy in our hearts, we bring great joy to Jesus. And that's what is desperately needed when we are depressed!

Main Point

The person who is depressed needs the joy of the Lord as their strength.

Questions for Reflection

- What is the greatest need of the person who is depressed?
- How is the 'joy of the LORD' our strength?
- Why do most people just settle for happiness rather than joy?
- What is keeping you from experiencing long-lasting joy right now?

Appendix A: What Now?

- Make a list of the 'outside' things that are pressing down on you right now. What things can you change , and which ones do you have to just accept?
- Think about where you are on the 'downward spiral' of depression. In what ways can you rightly respond in order to stop the descent?
- Are there things you are grieving the loss of? Make a list, and talk about them with the Lord and other trusted people.
- Recognize that your body could be contributing to your problem. What physical health habits need to change? Eating? Sleeping? Exercising?
- If you haven't had a recent physical or wellness exam, consider having one. You also may want to make an appointment

to talk with your medical doctor about the possible need for medication.
- Enlist the help of a Christian counselor or a pastor. Receiving wise counsel, as well as having regular accountability, is a must.
- If you are having suicidal thoughts, immediately speak with a parent, trusted friend, pastor, or Christian counselor. Do not delay!
- Speak with trusted friends and family about your struggle. You do not have to walk alone.
- As hard as it may be to pray, you need to cry out to God about how you are feeling. Bring your laments, your sorrows, and your pain to Him!
- Make a commitment to be regularly in God's Word, allowing God to speak to you by His Spirit. Read through the Psalms on a daily basis, as well as Paul's letters.
- Are you an active member of a Bible-preaching local church? We all need to be a regular part of the community of believers.
- Think about the 'hope and trust' lines. Have you crossed them? Ask God to grow your hope and trust.

Appendix A: What Now?

- Consider if you are really struggling with underlying anger or anxiety. Get some good biblical counsel on those issues.
- As much as you may want to withdraw, become isolated, and avoid all pain, resist that temptation. Keep running the race!
- If you are a Christian, you can persevere because of the preserving love of Christ in your life. Don't quit!

Appendix B: Other Resources on this Topic

BOOKLETS/MINI-BOOKS ON DEPRESSION

Ray, Bruce. *Help! My Friend is Suicidal (Lifeline mini-books)*. (Wapwallopen, PA: Shepherd Press, 2014)

Trahan, Carol. *Help! I'm Depressed (Lifeline mini-books)*. (Wapwallopen, PA: Shepherd Press, 2014)

Welch, Edward T. *Depression: The Way Up When You're Feeling Down* (Greensboro, NC: New Growth Press, 2012)

BOOKS ON DEPRESSION

Eswine, Zack. *Spurgeon's Sorrows: Realistic Hope for those who Suffer from Depression* (Fearn, Scotland: Christian Focus, 2015)

Lloyd-Jones, D. Martyn. *Spiritual Depression: Its Causes and Its Cure* (Grand Rapids, MI: Eerdmans, 1965)

Piper, John. *When the Darkness will not Lift: Doing what we can when we wait for God and Joy* (Wheaton, IL: Crossway, 2006)

_____. *When I Don't Desire God: How to Fight for Joy* (Wheaton, IL: Crossway, 2013)

Somerville, Bob. *If I'm a Christian, Why am I Depressed?* (Maitland, FL: Xulon Press, 2014)

Welch, Edward T. *Depression: Looking Up from the Stubborn Darkness* (Greensboro, NC: New Growth Press, 2011)

Watch out for other forthcoming books in the *Track* series, including:

Justification (2022)
Gaming (2022)
Worldview (2022)
Womanhood (2022)
Rest (2022)
Missions
Prayer
Body Image
Dating & Marriage
Music
Social Media
Apologetics

Reformed Youth Ministries (RYM) exists to reach students for Christ and equip them to serve. Passing the faith on to the next generation has been RYM's passion since it began. In 1972 three youth workers who shared a passion for biblical teaching to youth surveyed the landscape of youth ministry conferences. What they found was an emphasis on fun and games, not God's Word. Therefore, they started a conference that focused on the preaching and teaching of God's Word. Over the years RYM has grown beyond conferences into three areas of ministry: conferences, training, and resources.

- **Conferences:** RYM's youth conferences take place in the summer at a variety of locations across the United States and are continuing to expand. We also host

parenting conferences throughout the year at local churches.
- **Training:** RYM launched an annual Youth Leader Training (YLT) conference in 2008. YLT has grown steadily through the years and is offered in multiple locations. RYM also offers a Church Internship Program in partnering local churches as well as youth leader coaching and youth ministry consulting.
- **Resources:** RYM offers a variety of resources for leaders, parents, and students. Several Bible studies are offered as free downloads with more titles regularly being added to their catalogue. RYM hosts multiple podcasts: *Parenting Today*, *The Local Youth Worker*, and *The RYM Student Podcast*, all of which can be downloaded on multiple formats. There are many additional ministry tools available for download on the website.

If you are passionate for passing the faith on to the next generation, please visit www.rym.org to learn more about Reformed Youth Ministries. If you are interested in partnering with us in ministry, please visit www.rym.org/donate.

A Student's Guide to Technology

JOHN PERRITT

Technology can be a great gift. It allows us to communicate with people all over the world instantly. But it can also do great harm if not used wisely. This short book gives helpful suggestions for how to use technology to glorify God in our lives, as well as making us aware of what dangers there are in misusing technology.

978-1-5271-0449-5

LIGON DUNCAN & JOHN PERRITT

A STUDENT'S GUIDE TO
SANCTIFICATION

A Student's Guide to Sanctification

LIGON DUNCAN & JOHN PERRITT

Knowing that we have been saved by what Jesus has done rather than by what we have done is amazing. But how does this knowledge affect the way we live? What's the point in being good if we will be forgiven anyway? Actually the Bible says that God's forgiveness frees us to live for Him and through the Holy Spirit we can grow to become more and more like Jesus. Ligon Duncan and John Perritt dive into what that means in this short book.

978-1-5271-0451-8

EDWARD T. WELCH

A Student's Guide to Anxiety

EDWARD T. WELCH

We all know the feeling. That nervous, jittery, tense feeling that tells you that something bad is just ahead. Anxiety can be overwhelming. But the Bible has plenty to say to people who are anxious. This book will help us to take our eyes off our circumstances and fix them on God.

978-1-5271-0450-1

A Student's Guide to the Power of Story

Joe Deegan

Stories are powerful. They shape us and stay with us in a way that nothing else does. Ideas and wisdom can be portrayed in a way that draws the listener or reader in. Stories can build relationships and understanding. They can help to make sense of confusing concepts. In this compelling addition to the *Track* series, Joe Deegan explains why stories are so important – and what role they play in our everyday lives.

978-1-5271-0695-6

WALT MUELLER
SERIES EDITED BY
JOHN PERRITT

A STUDENT'S GUIDE TO NAVIGATING CULTURE

TRACK CULTURE

A Student's Guide to Navigating Culture

WALT MUELLER

We all belong to a culture. From the shows we watch to the language we use to the food we eat; culture shapes the way we look at the world, the way we act, the way we think. It affects so much of our lives, and yet we are rarely aware of it. If we are not careful, it can push us away from God's good desires for who we are and how we live in our world.

978-1-5271-0694-9

A Student's Guide to Glorification

Derek W. H. Thomas

In this short book for young adults, Derek Thomas explains what the Bible means when it talks about glory. Beginning with the Creation, he explains how the reflection of God's glory was not completely destroyed when sin entered the world, but it was broken. Thomas then goes on to explain how this glory of God was perfectly represented in the person of Jesus; how it is partially restored in Christians; and how it will be perfectly restored in the new heavens and the new earth.

978-1-5271-0694-9

Christian Focus Publications

Our mission statement —

STAYING FAITHFUL

In dependence upon God we seek to impact the world through literature faithful to His infallible Word, the Bible. Our aim is to ensure that the Lord Jesus Christ is presented as the only hope to obtain forgiveness of sin, live a useful life and look forward to heaven with Him.

Our books are published in four imprints:

CHRISTIAN FOCUS

Popular works including biographies, commentaries, basic doctrine and Christian living.

CHRISTIAN HERITAGE

Books representing some of the best material from the rich heritage of the church.

MENTOR

Books written at a level suitable for Bible College and seminary students, pastors, and other serious readers. The imprint includes commentaries, doctrinal studies, examination of current issues and church history.

CF4·K

Children's books for quality Bible teaching and for all age groups: Sunday school curriculum, puzzle and activity books; personal and family devotional titles, biographies and inspirational stories — because you are never too young to know Jesus!

Christian Focus Publications Ltd,
Geanies House, Fearn, Ross-shire,
IV20 1TW, Scotland, United Kingdom.
www.christianfocus.com
blog.christianfocus.com